AORAKI/MOUNT COOK

WITH THE CANTERBURY LAKES

Mounts Aoraki/Mount Cook and Tasman at sunset.

Larch trees in autumn at Lake Pukaki.

Photographs, text and design by

PETER MORATH

Printed and published by

THE CAXTON PRESS
PRINT & DESIGN

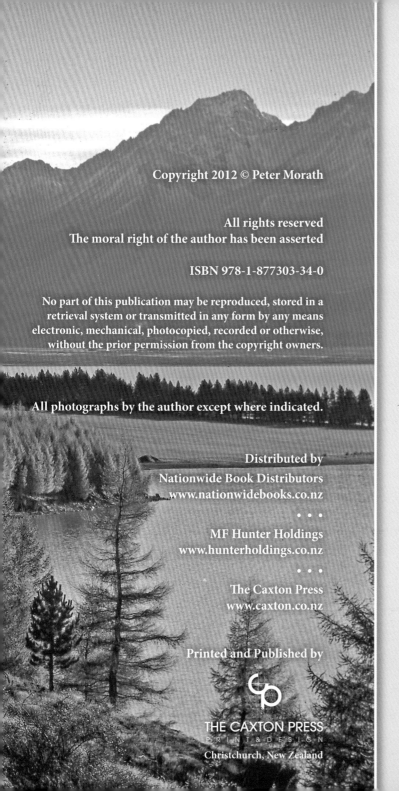

Copyright 2012 © Peter Morath

All rights reserved
The moral right of the author has been asserted

ISBN 978-1-877303-34-0

No part of this publication may be reproduced, stored in a retrieval system or transmitted in any form by any means electronic, mechanical, photocopied, recorded or otherwise, without the prior permission from the copyright owners.

All photographs by the author except where indicated.

Distributed by
Nationwide Book Distributors
www.nationwidebooks.co.nz

• • •

MF Hunter Holdings
www.hunterholdings.co.nz

• • •

The Caxton Press
www.caxton.co.nz

Printed and Published by

THE CAXTON PRESS
PRINT & DESIGN
Christchurch, New Zealand

AORAKI/ MOUNT COOK

WITH THE CANTERBURY LAKES

Left: Lake Pukaki and Aoraki/Mount Cook.

New Zealand's South Island

Aoraki/Mount Cook with Lake Pukaki.

Springtime at Lake Heron.

Europeans started to arrive in New Zealand in small numbers after James Cook's first landing in 1769, but it was not until the 1840s that European immigration began. Settlers found a wild and undeveloped land of great beauty and diversity. In the South Island great contrasts existed either side of the Main Divide, with lush rain forests to the west and and vast, dry plains to the east.

Since their arrival much has changed. The land has been tamed, large cities built and modern technology and communication introduced. While the jet-age has brought New Zealand much closer to the rest of the world, its geographic isolation has ensured that it remains virtually free of the atmospheric pollution of more populous continents. Its skies retain a rare clarity, enabling its scenic magnificence to be enjoyed to the full.

In 1842 Nelson became the South Island's first region to receive immigrants from Britain in large numbers. Much hard work was required to clear the land, but they had come to a bountiful area. Nelson and its neighbouring province of Marlborough enjoy more sunshine than anywhere else in the country. Today the region produces vines, fruit, hops and timber in abundance. Marlborough makes world class wines and the magic of its Sounds competes with Nelson's golden beaches to attract holiday makers.

The pace of life on the West coast is much more leisurely now than during the frenetic gold rushes of the 1860s. Timber is the main industry and coal is still mined, mainly for exporting. Greymouth and Westport have active fishing fleets, and there is farming along the coastal strip. The scenery has unique beauty, with the country's highest peaks reflected in calm lakes and verdant native bush sweeping down to meet the pounding surf of the Tasman Sea.

Canterbury, the country's largest province, lies to the east of the Main Divide. The strong contrast between the tussock-covered foothills and vast plains is immediately noticed by the visitor arriving from the forested west. This is farming country on a grand scale and, not surprisingly, agriculture is the largest of the region's diverse industries. Much of New Zealand's electricity is generated by the hydro lakes in the Mackenzie Basin in the south, above which tower some of the country's highest mountains. Christchurch is the provincial centre and the second largest city in the country. There the English influence is very strong, exemplified by such activities as punting on the Avon River.

The gold rushes of the 1860s reached their peak in the central areas of Otago. As a result, Dunedin became the most populated city in the country for a time. Today it is the second largest urban area

Left: Autumn at Lake Pukaki, with Aoraki/Mount Cook and Mount Tasman.

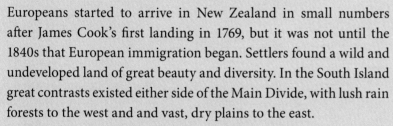

in the South Island, with a strong Scottish heritage and much fine Victorian architecture. The scenic peninsula nearby has the world's only mainland nesting site of the royal albatross. Queenstown is the island's main tourist destination with a strong emphasis on adventure activities. Central Otago has some magnificent mountain and lake scenery, which is seen at its glorious best clad in the gold of autumn.

Southland is another major farming region. Its main city of Invercargill is not far from a large aluminium smelter at Bluff, a port renowned for its oysters. Frequent ferry services operate from here to beautiful, unspoiled Stewart Island. The region also boasts the country's only World Heritage Area, the pristine Fiordland National Park.

New Zealand's population is currently about 4.5 million, under a quarter of whom live in the South Island. Maori are 15% of the total population, the majority in the North Island.

In this book we travel to Canterbury, New Zealand's largest and one of its most spectacular provinces. Firstly, we see the magnificent Aoraki/Mount Cook National Park and then move on to explore the more scenic of Canterbury's many beautiful lakes. I hope you enjoy your visit.

Peter Morath

Left: Lake Grasmere near Cass, Canterbury.

AORAKI/MOUNT COOK

The western side of the Main Divide with Mounts Aoraki/Mount Cook and Tasman in the centre.

Canterbury is very well endowed with mountains of stunning grandeur, most of which are in the centre and south of the region. The best known of these is Aoraki/Mount Cook (3754m), which is New Zealand's highest and is the centre piece of the wonderful National Park which bears its name. To reach it, take the Hermitage turn-off from State Highway 8 at Pukaki which provides one of the country's most scenic drives. The road skirts Lake Pukaki and leads into the National Park with the mountain looming ever larger as the road progresses, until approaching Mount Cook Village the scene is dominated by the majestic bulk of Mount Sefton towering above. There is much to see

and do in Aoraki/Mount Cook Village. One of the most sensational things for the visitor is a ski-plane flight onto the glaciers, the Tasman Glacier being the most popular of these. Grand circular flights can also be taken over the Southern Alps' highest peaks. The Hooker Valley track leads walkers to the base of Mount Cook itself and there are several other easy walking tracks. For the more experienced climbers and mountaineers there is endless opportunity to enjoy their sport. The visitor centre has many fine displays showing different aspects of this magnificent region. The historic Hermitage hotel provides top class accommodation.

Mustering rams at Glentanner Station with, in the background, Mount La Perouse to the left of Aoraki/Mount Cook.

An obligingly arranged flock at Glentanner Station.

Walking the Hooker Track alongside the Hooker River, Aoraki/Mount Cook at the end of the valley.

The Hooker Valley in mid-winter.

The great heights of Mounts Aoraki/Mount Cook (3754m) and Tasman (3497m) can be fully appreciated when seen from the southern end of Lake Pukaki.

Mounts La Perouse (3078m) and Aoraki/Mount Cook, seen from their western side in this aerial view.

Autumn sheep mustering on the road to The Hermitage.

Above: Cattle droving in Aoraki/Mount Cook National Park.
Following two pages: Wild Lupins in bloom in early summer at Glentanner, with Lake Pukaki and Aoraki/Mount Cook.

The Tasman Glacier, location for most of the ski-plane landings, Aoraki/Mount Cook in the centre.

Tourist boat on Lake Tasman, with icebergs from the glacier. Aoraki/Mount Cook in the background.

A Cessna 185 ski-plane on the Tasman Glacier. These aircraft have retractable skis and operate out of Aoraki/Mount Cook Airport.

Ski-plane flying over ice cliffs on the Tasman Glacier.

Two of Aoraki/Mount Cook National Park's most famous mountains. **Above:** Mount Sefton (3151m).
Left: Mount Malte Brun (3198m).

Wild lupins near The Hermitage with The Footstool peak, which is part of Mount Sefton.

Mount Cook lilies and wild foxgloves in Aoraki/Mount Cook National Park.

Above: Autumn in the National Park.
Right: Aoraki/Mount Cook at sunset looking north.

Above: Late evening reflections in a small tarn in the National Park.
Right: Aoraki/Mount Cook at sunset looking south, with the ice dome of Mount Tasman in the foreground.

Lake Camp, which is very close to Lake Clearwater near Mount Somers.

Lake Benmore, with its huge hydro dam, is the most southerly of Canterbury's lakes. Travelling north, the next major one is Lake Ohau to the west with its diminutive close neighbour Lake Middleton. Further north near Twizel is Lake Ruataniwha, a well known rowing location, after which comes Lake Pukaki with its strong connection with Aoraki/Mount Cook, described in the previous chapter.

Lake Tekapo with its brilliant turquoise water is about 30 minutes drive to the east. The Church of the Good Shepherd there is well known for the view of the lake from its window looking towards the snow-capped mountains. Like its neighbouring lakes, Pukaki and Ohau, Tekapo is part of a massive hydro-electric system in the Mackenzie Basin, the lakes being linked by wide canals.

Moving into the central area of Canterbury, Lakes Clearwater, Camp and Heron can be accessed from Mount Somers township, the drive taking about an hour. All are very scenic, Lake Heron arguably being the most attractive. The final parts of the roads to these are unsealed. Lake Coleridge can be reached from near Rakaia Gorge. State Highway 73 from Christchurch to the West Coast passes several lakes before crossing over Arthur's Pass. Small Lake Lyndon is on the left of the road at the top of Porters Pass and further along are Lakes Pearson, Sarah and Grasmere, the latter being the most attractive of the three, with its view towards Arthur's Pass National Park.

All of the country's fine lakes are best seen in either early spring or late autumn, when there is usually plenty of colour together with snow on the mountains which, on calm days, will be reflected in their placid waters. Early morning and late evening light will create longer shadows which help to show up the contours of the landscape.

Left: Lake Benmore from the air. Its hydro-dam and generating plant are in the foreground.

Lake Ruataniwha near Twizel, with its clear turquoise water, is a popular venue for rowing contests. Twizel is an excellent centre from which to explore the Aoraki/Mount Cook and Mackenzie Basin areas and has good accommodation.

Small but beautiful, Lake Middleton is very close to Lake Ohau in the south of Canterbury and near the North Otago border.

Pretty Lake Wardell is man-made and is close to the Aoraki/Mount Cook turn-off on State Highway 8. It makes a pleasant picnic place.

Lake Pukaki from its eastern side, with maple trees in their autumn brilliance making a colourful sight.

Above: The sculptured shoreline of Lake Tekapo wearing its winter garb.
Right: Snow emphasises the circular contours of Lake Alexandrina, Lake Tekapo's near neighbour.

Lake Tekapo, with the famous Church of the Good Shepherd.

Sunrise over Lake Tekapo.

The Maori Lakes near Mount Somers.

Springtime at beautiful Lake Heron, one of New Zealand's scenic gems, near Mount Somers.

Above: A winter muster on the banks of Lake Heron.
Left: Hot-air ballooning above the same lake.

Above: An aerial view of Lake Pearson with Lake Grasmere beyond. These lakes are near State Highway 73, one of the routes to the West Coast.
Left: Lake Camp near Mount Somers with Mount Potts.

Upper: Having fun in the snow at Lake Lyndon, near Porters Pass on State Highway 73.

Lower: Skating on Lake Clearwater near Mount Somers.

A calm day at Lake Grasmere, near Cass on the West Coast highway.

Lake Coleridge from the air. This is one of mid-Canterbury's best known lakes.